The Animated
ISRAEL
A HOMECOMING

Written by: Ephraim Sidon
Illustrations by: Hanan Kaminski
Gil Elkabetz

SCOPUS
FILMS

From the series
The Animated Holydays
Series Editor - Uri Shin'ar

Published by Scopus Films (London) Ltd.
P.O. Box 565, London N6 5YS
Suite 1102, 150 Fifth Avenue, New York, NY 10011
P.O. Box 8418, Jerusalem 91083

English version: Sam Orbaum
Educational editor: Udi Lion
Print production: David Melchior & Ehud Oren
Printed by: Omaney Dfus

Project producers: Uri Shin'ar & Jonathan Lubell
Made in Israel by Jerusalem Productions Ltd.,

ISBN 0—8246—0326—5

Distributors: USA — Jonathan David Publishers Inc.,
68-22 Eliot Avenue, Middle Village, NY 11379
UK — Kuperard (London) Ltd., P.O. Box 565, London N6 5YS

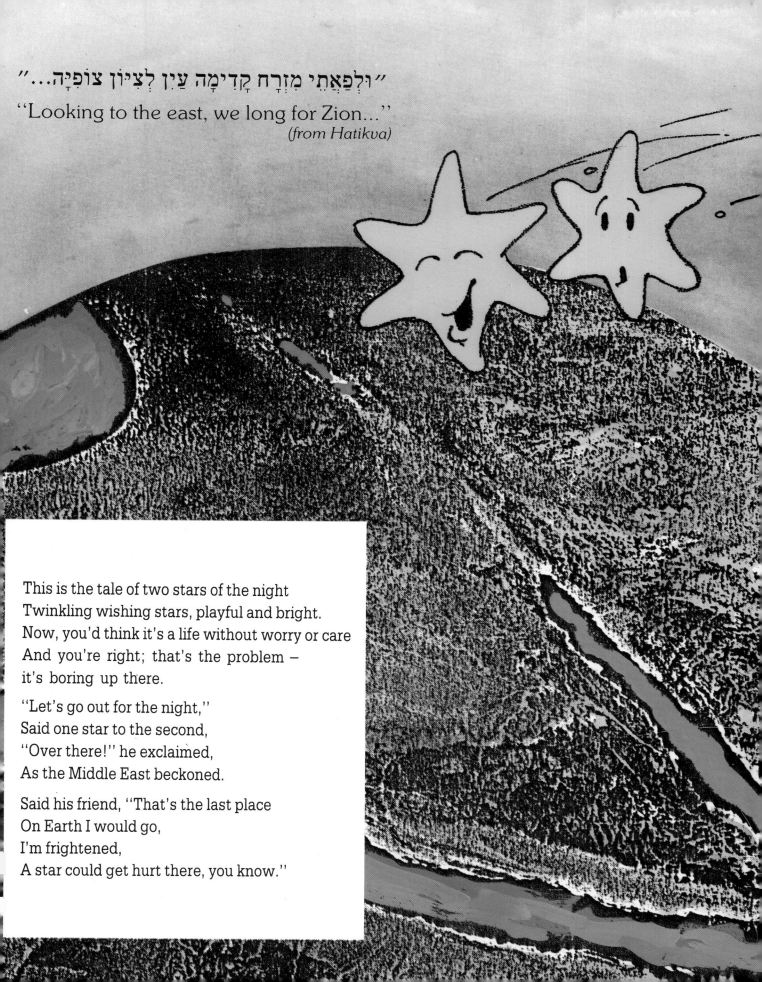

"וּלְפַאֲתֵי מִזְרָח קָדִימָה עַיִן לְצִיּוֹן צוֹפִיָּה..."

"Looking to the east, we long for Zion..."
(from Hatikva)

This is the tale of two stars of the night
Twinkling wishing stars, playful and bright.
Now, you'd think it's a life without worry or care
And you're right; that's the problem –
it's boring up there.

"Let's go out for the night,"
Said one star to the second,
"Over there!" he exclaimed,
As the Middle East beckoned.

Said his friend, "That's the last place
On Earth I would go,
I'm frightened,
A star could get hurt there, you know."

Said the first, "Don't be silly, there's nothing to fear,
They're happy and dancing and singing, I hear."
So they landed close by, and alit in a tree,
And parted its leaves all the better to see.

"It's a house!" "Yes I know, I have seen one before.
They're celebrating, let's stay a bit more."
Through a window they saw a happy young boy
Surrounded by people, all dancing for joy.

"L'Chaim! To life!" they cheered the young host
And each raised a glass in proposing a toast.
"Some kind of a party," the timid star said.
His friend only twinkled and nodded his head.

Then suddenly spoke a mysterious voice:
"A birthday it is, that's why they rejoice."
"Who's that? I heard someone! But who could it be?
There's just me and you, that house and this tree."

"הַיּוֹם יוֹם הֻלֶּדֶת"

"Happy birthday."
(children's song)

Said a voice from the tree, "Etz is my name.
A pleasure to meet you, I'm happy you came."
"A tree that can speak – that's utterly shocking!"
"You're right," said the tree, "but look who's talking!"

The three of them laughed, then the tree heaved a sigh;
And the stars sensed a sadness and asked the tree why.
"It's a very long story, both happy and sad –
If you had time to listen..." Said the stars, "We'd be glad!
Provided it doesn't take more than a night,
We have to get back before it gets light."

With a whoosh! whipped the wind like a magical spell;
Dear friends: here's the story that Etz had to tell...

"...אֶל אֶרֶץ זָבַת חָלָב וּדְבָשׁ..."
"...to a land flowing
with milk and honey..."
(Exodus Ch 3)

"It happened right here, some centuries past.
I was smaller back then, as the shadow I cast.
Nearby, people lived in a house made of clay,
And a boy and a girl, with whom I would play.
We also did work – we herded the sheep
And planted the crops, to harvest and reap.

"זָכַרְתִּי לָךְ חֶסֶד נְעוּרַיִךְ אַהֲבַת כְּלוּלֹתָיִךְ, לֶכְתֵּךְ אַחֲרַי בַּמִּדְבָּר."

"I remembered your kindness and love from long ago. Come follow me to the desert."

(Jeremiah Ch 2)

The other best friend, as you haven't yet heard,
Was a twittering, flittering, little gray bird.

We grew up together, our life seemed so good.
We cared for each other as best of friends should.

Whatever our worries or troubles or strife
We'd always stay true to each other for life!
And then just to prove that our friendship was sure,
We agreed to a pact that would always endure...

Midnight.
The bird, softly
Whistles...
The signal!
A secret meeting...
Four friends.
Friends for-
Ever.
The Covenant – the pact!
Ready?
The boy, the girl, the bird, the tree...
Together to
E-ter-ni-ty!

The bird plucked a feather,
A beautiful quill.
In the midnight moonlight,
The air so still;

Then I, in a moment
Solemn and brief,
Presented – as parchment –
My finest leaf.

The children carefully cut a lock of their hair,
To seal the pact we had all come to share.

"Upon our lives this promise we make
And hereby vow we shall never forsake.
This boy, this girl, this bird and this tree
Do solemnly swear: 'If I forget thee...' "

The pact was sealed and hidden together:
The locks of the children, the leaf and the feather.

"אִם אֶשְׁכָּחֵךְ יְרוּשָׁלָיִם תִּשְׁכַּח יְמִינִי."

"If I forget you Jerusalem,
may my right hand lose its skill."
(Psalm 137)

Our youthful days were gentle and sweet,
Through winter rains and summer heat.
We played and played, though never knowing
The chilly winds of change were blowing...

‏"קוֹל שׁוֹפָר שָׁמַעַתְּ נַפְשִׁי תְּרוּעַת מִלְחָמָה."‏

"I hear the sounds and trumpet of war."

(Jeremiah Ch 4)

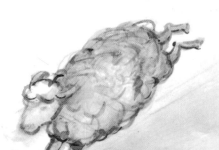

One day while playing hide-and-seek,
The bird swooped down, a wild gray streak.
"Danger approaches!" in horror she cried,
"The game is for real now – quick, children! Hide!"

Horses! Forces! Daggers and spears!
As frightening as the worst of our fears.
Crash! Destroy! Shatter! Smash!
They burned the little house to ash.

The children were safe, but others were not
With the house set ablaze they were easily caught.
They were carried away as we watched in despair,
We wanted to help but did not dare...

An angry invader,
A sneer on his face
Jabbed his spear
In their hiding place

"...קַלּוּ מִנְּשָׁרִים סוּסָיו, אוֹי לָנוּ כִּי שֻׁדָּדְנוּ."

"...his horses are faster than eagles, we have been destroyed."

(Jeremiah Ch 4)

Wrapped in my branches, the children were found
"Down!" he commanded. "Jump to the ground!"
He prodded them on to my shock and dismay:
"Hurry up, get a move-on – *you're going away*."
I shook in a rage and screamed to the sky
At the sight of the children waving goodbye.

The bird acted fast, in spite of her grief
And gave them our Covenant, wrapped in the leaf.
"Upon our lives this promise we make
And hereby vow we shall never forsake.
This boy, this girl, this bird and this tree
Do solemnly swear: 'If I forget thee...' "

"כְּצִפּוֹר נוֹדֶדֶת מִן־קִנָּהּ, כֵּן אִישׁ נוֹדֵד מִמְּקוֹמוֹ."

"As a bird that strays from its nest, so is a man wandering far from home."

(Proverbs Ch 27)

Suddenly, silence
Was thick in the air.
I couldn't believe
The children weren't there.
I asked the bird
To fly from the yard
To stay with our friends
And watch them, on guard.

From place to place
The children would wander
Throughout the world
From hither to yonder.
In Rome and in England,
From Russia to Spain
They flourished at first
Then wandered again.
The loyal gray bird
Would stay by their side
Then come back to me
To report and confide.

The bird had a message
Each time she returned:
"Next year in togetherness!"
Next year – still we yearned....

With the passage of time
New children appeared
They were nice, and we played,
But I still wasn't cheered.
I wistfully missed
The original four –
Oh, when would we be
Together once more?

The bird brought news,
I shouldn't complain;
"The news is good,
But ... let me explain:
They've settled down
At long, long last
Their days of wandering
For now are past.

But the pact it seems
Is not in their thoughts.
Now, Etz, understand,
And don't get in knots,
I'm sure when they're settled
We'll come back to mind
And the Covenant, too,
They so faithfully signed."

"לְבִּי בַּמִזְרָח וַאֲנִי בְּסוֹף מַעֲרָ

ough my heart is in the East, I find myself far
ay in the West."

(Rabbi Yehuda Halevi)

Years went by, disaster heightened,
I thought the world was more enlightened;
This Golden Age was not to be –
Our weary friends were forced to flee.

The bird then explained dispiritedly
"The boy and the girl are apart," said she.
"He has run off to Europe, to the west, to the north
She's south past the sea; I fly back and forth."

But worse was to come,
The most terrible yet,
I can't comprehend it;
I'll never forget...

The smoke and the fire
The evil machines
Death and destruction
By frightful means.

Somewhere consumed
In this horrible specter
The bird sought the boy
As his loyal protector.

The flames caught her wings
And in pain, shock and grief...
She found, not the boy
But only the leaf.

Weeping, she carried it home to me;
Her tears were so bitter she hardly could see.
I knew what had happened when I looked at her face
And we put the leaf back in its old hiding-place.

I waited and hoped for so long, but in vain;
I was sure I would not see the children again...

"לְשָׁנָה הַבָּאָה בִּירוּשָׁלַיִם."

"Next Year in Jerusalem"
(from the Haggadah)

"...הָבִיאִי בָנַי מֵרָחוֹק וּבְנוֹתַי מִקְצֵה הָאָרֶץ"

gather your sons and daughters from the
ds of the Earth."

(Isaiah Ch 43)

Our grief was still heavy when out of the blue
A woman approached whose features I knew.
At the very same moment I saw, not a boy,
But a man running hard and shouting for joy.
They were home! They were home! After so many years
We embraced in a flood of the happiest tears.
Said the bird, "Remember the pact we made:
Always together and never afraid."

We pitched in together, and each had a hand
In building a hut and reclaiming the land.
The bird flew to places far over the seas
And came back with seedlings to grow into trees.

The neighborhood children watched as they passed;
Some of them helped us, but most were aghast.

It took some time 'til I noticed, astounded:
The woman – my friend – was larger and rounded.
The bird noticed too, and she whispered to me
"I'm going to start calling you 'Grandfather Tree'!"

"שִׁיר, שִׁיר, עֲלֵה נָא, בַּפַּטִּישִׁים נַגֵּן נַגֵּנָה."

"We will sing a song while the hammers play
the tune."

(song by Natan Alterman)

Word got around of the pioneer pair
To family members living elsewhere.
They helped from afar, but then there were some
Who took up the call and decided to come.

But entry was barred to the homecoming kin,
An unfriendly soldier would not let them in.
(Sometimes they'd trick him, by catching his eye:
Distracted, he wouldn't see others slip by!)

"אַרְצָה עָלִינוּ."

"We came on aliyah."
(song by Shmuel Navon)

Listen! The sirens! Heading this way!
Nervous yet jubilant: this was the day!
All kinds of 'doctors' pushed their way through
Making a heck of a hullaballoo.
Uncle Sam, Mother Russia, Miss France – it was wild!
They all came to help in the birth of this child.

One shouted 'Yes!' and another said 'No!'
And another 'You can't!' And another 'Let go!'
It was such an event, this remarkable birth
It was broadcast on radio all over the Earth.

The family waited
As time trickled past...
Then the voice of a baby
Broke the silence at last.

"כֵּן... לֹא... נִמְנָע..."

"Yes... No... Abstain..."
(from the United Nations vote on creating a Jewish state)

The door of the hut
Was flung open wide
And we finally saw
What they'd come to decide...

"אָנוּ מַכְרִיזִים בָּזאת עַל הֲקָמַת
מְדִינָה יְהוּדִית בְּאֶרֶץ יִשְׂרָאֵל,
הִיא מְדִינַת יִשְׂרָאֵל."

"We declare the creation of a Jewish
country, that is the State of Israel."
*(from the Declaration of Independence,
read by David Ben Gurion)*

With a lump in my throat
 I managed to say,
"Yesterday's children
Are parents today!"

They gave me the child
And laid him to rest
In branches beside
The little bird's nest.

"This is Yisrael"
Said Papa so proud:
"He'll share in the pact
We so long ago vowed."

"... חַדֵּשׁ יָמֵינוּ כְּקֶדֶם."

"...renew our days as of old."
(from the prayer book)

The youngster learned to walk, and then run,
Playing with me as his parents had done.

Almost from when he had learned how to stand,
He took his first steps with a hoe in his hand.
The task was enormous, to rebuild the yard
But happy to help, we all worked hard.

The parents did not have to labor alone,
With family help we were not on our own.
Our needs were enormous, they well understood
And throughout the world they did what they could.

Yet many decided to come here to stay,
Arriving in every conceivable way...

Many arrived (this may sound absurd)
On wings of great eagles, amusing the bird!

Through deserts and swamps, via sea and by air
On rickety boats from goodness-knows-where.

On camels, on horseback,
On donkeys they came;
They travelled by foot
But arrived all the same.

Some even got here,
– I swear that it's true –
On "magical carpets"
That actually flew!

"...וְקָרֵב פְּזוּרֵינוּ מִבֵּין הַגּוֹיִם."

"...gather in our exiles from among the nations."
(from the prayer book)

Clearing the land, reviving the soil,
Such hard-working people, so happy to toil!

"נִבְנֶה אַרְצֵנוּ, אֶרֶץ מוֹלֶדֶת."

"Let us build up a nation, the land of our fathers."

(song by A. Levinson)

Where nothing had grown, now greenery bloomed
With farmland and gardens so lovingly groomed.
The hut was replaced with a new house of brick:
Then more and more houses – such progress, so quick!

At night we would camp
'Round a crackling fire
Singing to music
As flames fluttered higher;
Songs of the Russians,
Moroccans and British;
In French, Polish, Hebrew,
Ladino and Yiddish.

"...הִנֵּה מַה־טּוֹב וּמַה־נָּעִים שֶׁבֶת אַחִים גַּם־יָחַד."

"...it is good and pleasant to live together as brothers"
(Psalm 133)

But neighborhood children
Soon came into sight:
To get all the yard
They had come here to fight.

"מִסָּבִיב יֶהֱם הַסַּעַר..."

"As the battle rages around us.."

(the Palmach song)

"We were here first!" "Go away! It's my tree!"
"We'll fight you!" "I'm tougher!" "Sez who?" "Sez me!"

They punched and they kicked
And they cursed and they fought;
In horror I watched, and it made me distraught.
The children were many, little Yisrael one,
But fighting so bravely, he forced them to run.

But even in victory, Yisrael was sad
He didn't want enemies, but that's what he had.
"Why don't they like me? I want to be friends;
We shouldn't be fighting: we must make amends."
I tried to console him, to lighten his sorrow:
"The fighters today are the friends of tomorrow."

"לֹא־יִשְׂאוּ גוֹי אֶל־גּוֹי חֶרֶב וְלֹא־יִלְמְדוּן עוֹד מִלְחָמָה."

"Nation shall not lift up sword against nation and
they shall know war no more."

(Micah Ch 4)

The fighting was over
And life carried on
But working so much,
The sparkle was gone.

Building all day
With no time to be free,
It seemed he'd forgotten
The bird and me.

Like "grandparents" everywhere
We needed a smile.
Why can't he visit us
Once in a while?

"I don't understand," said the unhappy bird
"He simply neglects us, he won't say a word!"
Then spreading her wings, she kissed me goodbye,
And swiftly became just a dot in the sky.

Now I'm old and alone, and I'm sorry to say,
That although it is Yisrael's birthday today
I guess that I really feel happy and glad –
But missing my friends still makes me sad.

"יְרוּשָׁלַיִם שֶׁל זָהָב."

"Jerusalem of Gold."

(song by Naomi Shemer at the time of the six day war)

Well, stars, that's the story;
Now, before it gets light
There's much you can do
To brighten this night…

I have to stay here, as I'm only a tree;
You're able to fly, so maybe you'll see
Somewhere on Earth, this little gray bird
Look for her, find her; please give me your wo

In forests, on mountains, in valleys, at sea
They searched through the world so valiantly.
Tired and sad they returned to the yard:
"I'm sorry we failed, though we tried very hard."

Then all of a sudden a chirp could be heard
Startled, the stars and the tree saw – the BIRD!
At the very same moment, the boy came outside
"My friend has come back!" little Yisrael cried.

"הֵבֵאנוּ שָׁלוֹם עֲלֵיכֶם."
"We have brought peace to you."
(song by Yossi Gamzu and Sasha Argov)

"My gift," said the bird, "no other could give –
A neighborhood child, with whom you can live."
Then out of the shadows the youngster appeared,
Shook Yisrael's hand as the rest of us cheered.

"Salaam, Yisrael..." "Shalom," he replied;
"We are all here to celebrate – join us inside!
Come in and share in the wish I shall make
When the candles go out on my birthday cake."

Said Etz with a wink,
"You stars have a duty!
Shoot through the sky,
Let them wish on your beauty."

"So long," said the stars, "We are ready to go;
We've had a great night. Now – look out below!"

They streaked through the sky in a dazzling show
And Yisrael's face lit up from the glow.
He whispered a wish, that only he knew...
But someday – you'll see – his wish will come true.

"... הַתִּקְוָה בַּת שְׁנוֹת אַלְפַּיִם."

"...the hope of two thousand years."

(from Hatikva)

The Animated HOLYDAYS

An entertaining and educational series of children's books, films and games on the Jewish festivals.

OTHER TITLES:

Rosh Hashanah — The Animated Year book and Calendar.

Hannukah — The Animated Menorah book and "Hannukit" gift box.

Purim — The Animated Megillah book.

Pesach — The Animated Haggadah book and video-cassette.

What the critics say:

"The perfect gift for a child...fantastic illustrations." (New York Times)

"The whole enterprise has a charm and freshness all of its own." (Jewish Chronicle)

"Very appealing...wonderful storybook..." (Jerusalem Post)

"The traditional family seder will never be quite the same..." (Electronic Media)

"A tremendous production...artistic quality in both content and presentation." (Israel Broadcasting Service)